Reptile World

Death Adders

by Imogen Kingsley

Bullfrog
Books

Ideas for Parents and Teachers

Bullfrog Books let children practice reading informational text at the earliest reading levels. Repetition, familiar words, and photo labels support early readers.

Before Reading

- Discuss the cover photo. What does it tell them?

- Look at the picture glossary together. Read and discuss the words.

Read the Book

- "Walk" through the book and look at the photos. Let the child ask questions. Point out the photo labels.

- Read the book to the child, or have him or her read independently.

After Reading

- Prompt the child to think more. Ask: Death adders are venomous. What other snakes can you think of that are venomous?

Bullfrog Books are published by Jump!
5357 Penn Avenue South
Minneapolis, MN 55419
www.jumplibrary.com

Library of Congress Cataloging-in-Publication Data

Names: Kingsley, Imogen, author.
Title: Death adders / by Imogen Kingsley.
Other titles: Bullfrog books. Reptile world.
Description: Minneapolis, MN: Jump!, Inc., [2017]
Series: Reptile world
"Bullfrog Books are published by Jump!."
Audience: Ages 5-8. | Audience: K to grade 3.
Identifiers: LCCN 2016050981 (print)
LCCN 2016051804 (ebook)
ISBN 9781620316665 (hard cover: alk. paper)
ISBN 9781624965432 (e-book)
Subjects: LCSH: Acanthophis—Juvenile literature.
Elapidae—Juvenile literature. | CYAC: Snakes.
Classification: LCC QL666.O64 K5627 2017 (print)
LCC QL666.O64 (ebook) | DDC 597.96/4—dc23
LC record available at https://lccn.loc.gov/2016050981

Editor: Kirsten Chang
Book Designer: Molly Ballanger
Photo Researcher: Molly Ballanger

Photo Credits: Joel Sartore/Getty, cover, 24; fivespots/Shutterstock, 1, 3; Martin Willis/Minden Pictures, 4; Stewart Macdonald, 5; Auscape/Getty, 6–7; TED MEAD/Getty, 7; Michael & Patricia Fogden/SuperStock, 8–9; reptiles4all/Thinkstock, 10; Ken Griffiths/Photoshot, 11, 16–17, 18–19; Morales/SuperStock, 12–13; A.N.T. Photo Library/ Photoshot, 14; Shcherbakov Ilya/Shutterstock, 15; Jade ThaiCatwalk/Shutterstock, 16–17; Maik Dobiey, 20–21; Gerry Pearce/Alamy Stock Photo, 22; Joe McDonald/Shutterstock, 23br.

Printed in the United States of America at Corporate Graphics in North Mankato, Minnesota.

Table of Contents

A Fast Strike

What is in the leaves?

It is a death adder!

These snakes
are hard to see.

Some look like leaves.

Some look like sand.

They hide.

They wait for prey.

They may wait for days!

How do they sense prey?

They see.

They smell.

They feel the
ground move.

Look!

Here comes a rat.

The snake moves his tail.
It looks like a worm.

tail

The rat sees it.

She moves closer.

The snake strikes.
He is very fast!
It takes less
than a second.

17

He bites.

Venom comes
out of his fangs.

The rat dies.

The snake is full.

It is time to rest.

Parts of a Death Adder

body
Death adders have short, thick bodies that are patterned to camouflage them in the wild.

head
Death adders have big, triangular heads.

tail
A death adder's tail can be colorful or plain black. It acts like a lure, shaking to attract prey.

fangs
A death adder injects venom with its fangs.

Picture Glossary

prey
Animals that are hunted for food.

strikes
Attacks.

sense
To feel, see, hear, smell, taste, or to be aware of something.

venom
Liquid poison.

Index

To Learn More

Learning more is as easy as 1, 2, 3.

1) Go to www.factsurfer.com

2) Enter "deathadders" into the search box.

3) Click the "Surf" button to see a list of websites.

With factsurfer.com, finding more information is just a click away.